WILD & FREE

Poetry of Living, Loving & Letting Go

Be wild + free!

SHERRY SADOFF HANCK

BALBOA PRESS
A DIVISION OF HAY HOUSE

Copyright © 2019 Sherry Sadoff Hanck.

All rights reserved. No part of this book may be used or reproduced by any means, graphic, electronic, or mechanical, including photocopying, recording, taping or by any information storage retrieval system without the written permission of the author except in the case of brief quotations embodied in critical articles and reviews.

This book is a work of non-fiction. Unless otherwise noted, the author and the publisher make no explicit guarantees as to the accuracy of the information contained in this book and in some cases, names of people and places have been altered to protect their privacy.

Balboa Press books may be ordered through booksellers or by contacting:

Balboa Press
A Division of Hay House
1663 Liberty Drive
Bloomington, IN 47403
www.balboapress.com
1 (877) 407-4847

Because of the dynamic nature of the Internet, any web addresses or links contained in this book may have changed since publication and may no longer be valid. The views expressed in this work are solely those of the author and do not necessarily reflect the views of the publisher, and the publisher hereby disclaims any responsibility for them.

The author of this book does not dispense medical advice or prescribe the use of any technique as a form of treatment for physical, emotional, or medical problems without the advice of a physician, either directly or indirectly. The intent of the author is only to offer information of a general nature to help you in your quest for emotional and spiritual well-being. In the event you use any of the information in this book for yourself, which is your constitutional right, the author and the publisher assume no responsibility for your actions.

Any people depicted in stock imagery provided by Getty Images are models, and such images are being used for illustrative purposes only. Certain stock imagery © Getty Images.

Print information available on the last page.

ISBN: 978-1-9822-2321-2 (sc)
ISBN: 978-1-9822-2338-0 (e)

Balboa Press rev. date: 03/28/2019

Dedication

Dedicated to my great-niece Ella Rose, the first of her generation. First born of my sister's first born who was my mother's first born (who was also first born). And so it begins again …

Acknowledgements

I acknowledge

the profound loss of my beloved father, who lives in my breathing, beating heart

my precious mother who is facing her ending with grace and humor

the challenging moments for the wisdom they deliver

the value of community and importance of solitude

family, friends & pets

good food, great talent & wondrous wanderings

the essential role of laughter in trying times

I acknowledge that love is my foundation and that without its True North, I would be lost

Introduction

This collection, Wild & Free, is not so much about the continuity of themes throughout the poems, rather its flavor is derived from the time in which it was written.

The two years that span the time this collection was composed, were heavy in lessons of impermanence. I saw the inside of more hospitals in this time than I have in the whole of my 50 years.

Living
Loving
Letting Go

This is the cycle we are in from inhalation to exhalation, waking to sleeping, birth to death. Creation as the portal to living – Loving, as an expression of preservation – Letting Go as the inevitable dissolution of that life, big or small.

Contents

Wise Words by, Robert L. Sadoff, MD (2/8/1936 – 4/17/2017) 1
Writing Free 2
Harmony 3
Ode to Joe ~ from his Pepper Pot (or The Business of Family) 4
Uncomfortable Truth 7
We Know 8
Stars & Stripes 10
Sing 12
In Rogue, Not Vogue 13
No Space for Hate – Just Space 14
Uncertain Trust 16
Grace 17
Cancer Chronicles 18
The Mirror 20
Passing Time 22
Heavy 24
Breath by Breath 25
It's the Breath 26
Elf Days 28
Truth 29
Free Falling 30
Sky's the Limit 31
Radical Friendship 32
Believe 34

Boiling Point	35
Many Paths	36
Dig Deep	38
Callouses	39
Variations on a Theme	40
Fire Walk	42
Seduction	43
Moon Dance	44
Ripe, Red & Juicy	45
Thoughts on Paper	46
Why Are We Here?	47
No Bullshit	48
Auntie EM – [Word Purists Beware] (1:42am)	49
Wild & Free	50
Fertile Soil	51
Namaste	52
Fiery Sky	53
Hearts & Hands	54
On Our Island	55
Bodhisattva	56
Heat	57
Thank You	58
Light the Way	59
Watch Hand	60
Ding!	61
Past is Present	62
What's in a Moment?	63
Untamed	64
Who am I?	65
Body Muse	66
Guided by Voices	68
Be Happy, Take Five	69
Perspective	70
Wild Thing	72

Break a Leg	73
Bleeding	74
Awakening	76
Shadow Diving	77
Political Theatre	78
Fall	79
Pocono Lake	80
The Heart of Beauty	82
PART 1: Still Life Performance Art	84
PART 2: Still Life Performance Art	86
Have Courage	87
Living Mystery	88
Book Smart	89
Tick Tock	90
Aunt Gail	92
Capture	94
Generosity	95
Love	96
How to Say It	97
How to Say It	98
Presence	99
Good Grief	100
Freedom	101
Body	102
-Ism Shmism	103
Blowing in the Breeze	104
The Language of Feeling	105
Don't Give Your Power Away	106
Fandom	107
Love's Power	108
Seat of the Student	109
Enchantment	110
Union	111
United We Stand	112

Three Doors ~ past portals to future findings	114
Scratch Paper	116
Love Light	118
Speak Your Truth & Lighten the Load	120
(That's Not) Charlotte	122
Being Present	124
Space	125
Flow	126
Inspiration	127
Spoiler Alert	128
Love (un)Defined	130
House Blessing	131
White Coat	132
Stop	134
Jezebel	135
Grisping	136
Protest Song	137
Quest	138
Have Courage	139
Celebrating a Birthday in Heaven, Here on Earth	140
Love is…	141
80/50 thirty years	142
New Traditions	143
Spring Snow	144
Marble	145
When Words Fail	146
Shake it Out	147
What Lies Beneath	148
High Frequency	149
Tick Tock	150
Waiting for Spring	151
Fuck	152
Lost in Thought	153
Role Playing	154

Breezy	155
What's for Breakfast?	156
Keep Walking	157
April 17, 2018	158
Coin Toss	160
Heaven at Home	161
Technicolor Life	162
Water	164
The Once & Future…	165
Earth Song	166
The Gift of Emptiness	167
Knots	168
Giving & Receiving	170
Lighten Up	171
Nature's Secrets	172
What is the Purpose of a Porcupine?	174

Wise Words by, Robert L. Sadoff, MD (2/8/1936 – 4/17/2017)

*At a certain age
all we have to give
is our presence
and a hand to hold*

Writing Free

Unrestrained by
convention
rules & aesthetics
tastes of others'
imaginations

I drop the veil
grab my pen
and write

Harmony

I've no use of a small mind
        that remains tethered to
        stale notions
It clips the wings of growth, circling its one note

I've no interest in a single guru
        one voice singing solo of
        beliefs rooted in untended soil
It stagnates curiosity & tamps down imagination

The choir is much more interesting to me
four distinct lines
        one harmonious sound
reflecting and refracting
honoring the whole in
        all its parts

Ode to Joe ~ *from his Pepper Pot (or The Business of Family)*

From one generation to the next
We leave bread crumbs of wisdom
    and our missteps
        If we're lucky, the birds of our minds and habits don't
        eat them up
            before we can follow their trail to our highest
            selves

My grandparents blazed a path
and lit the way for so many
    Enriching lives too many to count
        Echoes of the opportunities they gave voice to
            reverberate in the heart of all they treasured

Clear and strong but never mean
my grandfather, Joe, was
    in the business of building up
        not tearing down

His structures
Labors of love
    were constructed of
        Character
        Generosity
            Loyalty & Expansion

Success, he would say, was a product of
    Reason
        Reality &
            Vision
He had all three.

I sifted through the artifacts of his office
Fingers black from wading through
    dozens of carbon paper documents, each in triplicate
        articles, letters and business cards galore
            revealing a meaningful, mission-driven life
            fully lived and cherished

Trash bags of shredded bank statements
dating back to the 1950s
    and other sensitive papers piled high
        Calendars and company business transactions
            became foliage to the mountain of dreams
            I was climbing

Inside a desk drawer I discovered a clean undershirt
neatly folded and pristine.
    Surrounded by the accumulated dust
        of many years, it shined like a beacon

I sat daydreaming about long nights
he must have spent at the office
    solving the puzzles of his business dealings
    conjuring new ways to build, create, give back
Business was his metaphor for life
    It was his super power and the way he communicated with the world
        I imagined him meeting every challenge with his
            confidence, smile and deep chuckle

What of that white undershirt?
Its simple significance secreted away – a story untold

"My Pepper Pot" grandpa would call me
    as I challenged his proper manner
        flying into his arms for a big hug

"Dear Girl" I could hear him say
"Be good to yourself" as he twirled a
    fork-full of Fettuccini Alfredo
        and took a bite

Uncomfortable Truth

Love is not always soft and
filled with chocolate and rose petals
It is often fierce and direct
uncomfortable in the way that it
wakes one up to the stark beauty and
truth of a thunder storm or
    sad splendor of a pierced *heart*
    We map out a *chart*
    A simple work of *art*
    It's a *start*

It requires courage to
show up every day to the
often raw emotions that link us to
the depths of our own tribe and
travel to the unknown territories of
    distant landscapes of *thought*
    It's the right we *bought*
    What we're *taught*
    Directing us to what we *sought*

Don't despair by what you see
Dive deeper into the pool of knowing
Trust the divine inside
I love you as you struggle to
scratch your way out of the
    cocoon of life's habitual hamster *wheel*
    It's the work you cannot *steal*
    That is the *deal*
    It's how I *feel*

We Know

We are a glimpse
a *glimmer*
a sparkle
a *shimmer*

before we *blink*
take a breath
clear our vision
have time to *think*

We Know

We know from
deep in the *space*
the Universe was born
out of solid *grace*
reflections of our
truest selves
from formless soul
to full-framed *face*
what is right and
what is *not*
how we act
from our own *spot*

Now is our promise
not *tomorrow*
each day's lot of
joy and *sorrow*
cannot be delayed or

put *away*
but must be dealt with
every *day*

Our brief time
upon this *earth*
is a contract signed
before our *birth*
Scorch the madness of
intolerance and *hate*
be the goodness
don't *berate*
be the one to
ardently *love*
to purify from *above*
the fray & tangle
of deceit
stand firm
stay true
liberate
redirect the course
don't rest in *fate*
Though our voices be
strong
We may not have
long
still, from love,
we must all
pollinate

Stars & Stripes

The disgrace is not in the burning of a flag
but in the active trashing of the ideals it represents
Dissent is a hallmark of freedom and should be
celebrated not vilified
        We focus on the wrong things
Get worked up over language not content
form not function
Our sensitive triggers ignite a maelstrom of reactions
from harsh words to sharp swords
        We raise our collective battle cries of injustice, they
echo
echo
echo
through empty minds and vacant hearts
searching for a place to land, absorb
be heard
        Sadly, we are deaf to each other's pleas
not the volume with which we tell the story
nor the facts that mesh with its telling
can be heard over the din of self-righteousness
        Our flag
Stars & Stripes
Strands of courage & unity, freedom, perseverance, resilience
Memories of those who fought – and continue to fight
for our Constitution, our Independence
        these strong but delicate fibers that bind our ideals so that
we may stand united and
not fall divided
        When the ideals that give the flag meaning are being
        pillaged

the act of burning it shows the deepest respect for its purpose
From its cinders, new fibers emerge to
weave the thread of what was lost into a new
vision
        worth fighting for

Sing

Sometimes I feel like a lyric searching for a tune
melody
harmony
rhythm
some vibrational delivery system to
release me into the world
not just to be heard but
to be sung

In Rogue, Not Vogue

Be your own taste maker
trust your inner guide
fasten your spiritual belt
choose which road and
take the ride!

Whether you opt the road not taken
or the one that's been well-trodden
commit to what dwells in your heart
and your path will surely broaden

When met with dissent along the way
from those who define what's vogue
smile or laugh as you reveal your truth
what's hip is now what's rogue

No Space for Hate – Just Space

I don't really hate cleaning
washing dishes
organizing
It's the anticipation
the mere thought that
moves my mind and
hands
away from the tasks and
into more desirable landscapes of
imagination

Once I'm in it
I actually like it
Swaying to tunes while
sweeping, moving things around
to the beat of the dance
Softening to the moment when
warm soapy water froths
blurring distinction
caressing
cleansing
what's in its path, creating a
sparkling tower

It's often like that
with tasks I dread
In their doing
they contain something joyful
and when completed

there's something of a satisfaction that
leads into the silence which follows

Time is a vacuum
suctioning life's grime into its own
container, while I do the same for the
filth I create
What is left is space
Space
to fill with creation and waste to
one day clear again to make more
space

Uncertain Trust

How do I start?
Take the first
       step
Heel-toe my way through the maze
Pay attention to the signs and hope they
make sense

It feels so big
I must break it down into
neighborhoods
Travel the back roads
Make note of the landmarks
       distinguishing aspects
All the while knowing
what seems sturdy, permanent
will transform with time

Once upon this moment
       is the beginning of
the story I will one day tell
myself

Grace

There is beauty
where there is suffering
it shows up in the formless acts of grace
that surround us always

Glaring
Staring
Seeing
into the relentless eyes of mortality
while digging deep
to find the strength
to fight the
good fight
one more day

Cancer Chronicles

We do not know each other stories
but that each story began with an inhalation
and will end with an exhalation

The deep groan
a reminder there's a human being
behind the pristine curtain
an audible reminder of suffering
Every curtain tells a tale

While you wait for your loved one
to emerge from behind her screen
you look around
> see the smudge marks of sneakers that once paced these halls
> feel the mental & physical strain of all who patiently wait
> smell the mingling of cafeteria food with unknown scents of

body odor
antiseptic cleaners
mad science medicines

Your senses become one entity
unable to distinguish one agony from another

The weight lightens enough for
giggles to escape the web of tension
woven from worry
The giggles grow

Laughter turns to tears without warning
A nurse you just met
but who feels like family
takes you under her cape and hugs you with her
angel wings

The Mirror

If you see the devil in someone else
turn your gaze inward
the heat of that insight is ignited
from within
The struggle to know oneself often
masquerades in judgements of others
these words do not live outside myself
they are echoes of living lessons
Every moment designed to dive
deep into the waters of
reflection
what stares back is not always
pretty or expected
rational or understood
Waking up is a choice
uncomfortable
complicated
salty and often
bitter
Eyes wide inward
we blink it back
alternating between
light and dark
open and shut
Vulnerable to the arrows of
nasty words and ignorance
I dig deep into my arsenal for the
love and discernment that are
my shield
Chinks in my armor

are the scars of my choices
rough patches on the smooth surface
touchstones of reality as seen
in my own reflection

Passing Time

Among the rumpled bed clothes
wires
apparatus
lies my precious father
thick tube down his throat
enabling him to breathe

At first his body reacts
thrashing
eyes open
distress
The nurse works fast to get the
proper dose of medicine in his system
for him to relax around
this foreign object

Following the longest minute
he calms
finding ease and finally
surrender

The tube carries the life-sustaining elixir
The big one
his breath
keeps his life force flowing
while he sleeps
Blue dye stains his skin
his chest rises and falls
to the rhythm of the
mechanical beeps

His hearing aids are perched in
his ears, which also sleep
I see the cuffs
binding his wrists to the bed
preventing him from removing the
breathing tube
and then my attention shifts to the
shiny watch on his wrist
ticking time as the new
pacemaker keeps his
heart ticking

The presence of the watch
disturbs me

These moments cannot be measured
by the relentless movement of the
second hand
The timepiece
a reminder of "to do" lists
and getting things done
seems both meaningless and
contrived

I sit by his side
Mom, exhausted in the chair
Deva Premal chants
Mantras for Precarious Times
lending us her voice
a melody line
providing a more palatable way
to pass this time

Heavy

Heavy and thick
      my bones
      the air
      my heart

the long hallways
lined with doors
rooms containing stories
white walls stained by time
smudged with the
grime of grief

Florescent lights
reveal every blemish
eyes held up by dark circles
cheeks streaked with tears of sorrow
hands quivering from uncontained spirit

laughter and joy
vibrate inside a sterilized
petri dish
creating an invisible dome
under which we gather to
hold the love

Breath by Breath

Short and shallow
yet constant and steady
Breath
labored by the fluid in his lungs
continues to animate his frail form
for an unknown length of time

We are all temporal
actively living or passively posing
stirred by our breath
deep diving
surface splashing
flailing, falling
resilient, rising
We connect through this breath
for an unknown length of time

It's the Breath

Give me the strength of spirit to
rise to the occasion of
my highest vibration

In those moments of truth
when anger, envy and fear begin to rise
If I'm lucky enough to have a pinhole of clarity
I get to make a choice

Do I follow the flow & frequency of the
wild water & rapids that keep it moving
as its momentum increases beyond control
OR
Do I take a breath, slow down
and see what happens?

Can a simple breath smooth the edges of
raw reaction?
Can it release my clenched fists and remind me
that my higher self sits perched on a hard stool –
the one next to the cushy throne occupied by
indulgence and separated self?
Will I choose to take that breath and risk the calm it promises?

The view from highest frequency is spectacular
It reveals communities of individual dots
When connected they create a mountain of unity
visible only from the apex of awake-ness

The climb is steady and long
requiring eyes open to its wonder
Unguarded hearts standing sentry at the base
Buoyancy and courage beckoning the breath
Ascending to surrender

Elf Days

Farewell sweet elf
whose time on our shelf
was brief when all's told
but was wily & bold

The longest day's gone
in light we move on
no regret & no fear
into this new year

Truth

Through the fog of
          perception
I see

No right
          No wrong
Veracity

What is truth
          but what
we think

Made from fact
          we extract
and drink

It pays to pause
          consider
more

Thoughts may shift
          not like
before

Free Falling

When I fall from grace
will the drop be long
enough to write an ode
or sing a song

Is it destiny
to take that ride
or fate that says
you never lied

this human thing
is not so simple
what seemed so smooth
now has a dimple

the best thing
that I can ask
is to mindfully
fulfill my task
        to question to
        my heart's delights
        not just what soothes
        but also frights

If I should free-fall
onto my face
at least I'll know
my start was grace

Sky's the Limit

Shake things up
Stretch your mind
Stillness waits
Search and find

Meet yourself
Where you are
Here and now
You're not too far

Rise above
Reach up high
There are no limits
Beyond the sky

Radical Friendship

Wandering through the collective memory of
lifetimes past
here we are
Reliving the highlights reel
mourning & celebrating the conflicts that created
the rich soil from which we now grow
flourish
blossom

Did we recognize each other from the start or
was the connection exposed through the
random acts of radical friendship
illustrative of our current incarnation

Enchantment is spun from the threads of our differences
made from the silky similarities of our hearts
weaving a cloth dynamic in color and pattern
It is a model for how to navigate a sleepy world
striving for disparate footholds to express isolated truths

We smash that paradigm
with smiles and sledge hammers
poised
we raise our sugar-rimmed martini glasses
bringing them down
shattering the glass veil of illusion

Our mission
styled by silliness

crafted in kindness
supported by the Universe
trails us wherever (and whenever)
we go

Believe

Do you believe in magic?
Signs from a Universe
tapping you on the mind
tugging at your heart
talking in living metaphors

"Wild & Free" it says
etched in the clear, smooth glass
butterflies of many colors
flitter around the curves
messengers of the moment

And then an actual butterfly
lackluster in color but
vibrant with meaning
flies in the door

Boiling Point

So this is what it feels like
        water when it's beginning to boil
simmering
        past the point of calm or choice
        momentum stirs the lulling rapids
        into action
The once still reflective surface
        bubbling in distortion
                is clear
What was just a dream now
        takes form
        as vapor rising

Many Paths

If words are all you have
be the author of your story
poetry
myth
fairytale

If action is your way
Inspire with heart-driven deeds
teaching
giving
doing

If music is your muse
compose your symphony
sing your song
play your heart
dance between the notes

If you are living in confusion
open to the light of
possibilities
revelations
insights

If your shadow appears
greet it with love
be the scribe
act from kindness
harmonize with others

Rest in its ephemeral coolness
Rising to each occasion

*Inspired by MLK's words, "If you can't fly then run, if you can't run then walk, if you can't walk then crawl, but whatever you do you have to keep moving forward." – He understood that we are all on different places on our paths and that whatever tools we have right now are enough, as long as we don't stall.

*Also inspired by a deep desire to work from a place of lifting up rather than knocking down. Honor your gifts (unique or common) and use them ~ you are not meant to keep them to yourself!

Dig Deep

If you allow another's view to
plant seeds of doubt on your path
yank those weeds with your own hands

Among your many talents
you are the gardener

Callouses

It's like a scab
I can't stop picking
the hard shell
protecting the
soft, fleshy place where
vulnerability lurks beneath the surface

Blood pools looking for release
seeping out from the edges
Poked, but not directly pierced

I scratch at this new itch
creating openings for my
life's essence to trickle out

This is what happens when
clarity & arrogance converge
certainty & self-righteousness
separate me from my pack

My softer spots harden under the
harsh light of smugness
leaving me calloused

Variations on a Theme

Self-righteousness is a bully
to the ideals that created it
What was once pure and good
can easily be corrupted by sanctimonious
ramblings of a hierarchical nature
creating a morality caste system

Words have the power to turn
from healing to hurting
becoming weapons in an
ideological war that cannot
be won

Those wielding these munitions
often dig their heels into the
soft soil of self-satisfaction
not realizing the harm
inflicted upon the earth and
Beings that inhabit it

This may be the crossroads where
clarity crosses swords with certainty
marking the start of an eternal conflict
where arrogance wears the crown

If we can spot the seed before it's planted
or yank the weed once it's grown
we may have a chance
not to win a battle of sides divided
but to gain enough common ground

A new terrain where we
collectively cultivate seeds that will
grow a diverse garden of flora
nourishing future generations with
the unity necessary to tend such a plot

It may not be the Eden of old
yet may hold capsules of enlightenment
miniature fruits of knowledge that will
lead us from the dark space of
ignorance and fear
into the bright rays that
light our way to understanding

Fire Walk

I refuse to get sucked into the nihilistic abyss

Life holds its challenges for us to meet
to grow beyond the places of comfort we seek
to become better versions of ourselves
even if it means walking through a scalding fire

Transformation is happening
burning fields to the ground for new growth

While on the other side of the fiery embers and choking smoke
we are breaking through our collective chrysalis
wings singed by the flames meant to purify us

Sailing smoothly
Flying free
on the clean current beyond the haze

Seduction

Seduce me not with the opulence of riches but
with the treasures of an open heart and
my knees will bend to the ground in reverence

Tantalize my tastes not with exotic fare but
with savory songs and sweet nothings and
we will dine on an eternity of tenderness

Tempt me not with grand gestures and empty promises but
with future memory joining heaven and earth
adventures of spirit will be the dirt under our fingernails

Moon Dance

Under a waning moon
the increasing darkness
frees me from the
bondage of
scrutiny
softens my deep smile lines
but does not dim the
sparkle in my eyes

The diminishing aperture
holds a light of its own
Beholding the gradually
darkening moon is an invitation
to full authentic being

How would you move your body
Express your urgency
Respond to the moment
under the shadow of the moon
Silhouetted by nature's sky-drop
left to shape, sound and movement
without the distraction of detail
I bathe in the beams of discovery
and dance in the moon's magical glow

Ripe, Red & Juicy

I love the color of raspberries when they're ripe
soaked in red by nature's favor
a hue so rich it trembles
moving the senses
like the mind
to take it all in

I love the texture of raspberries when they're ripe
gently touching the surface
bumpy but smooth
knowing beneath the surface
lies a succulent depth
one can only know
by taste

I love the taste of raspberries when they're ripe

Thoughts on Paper

Playing
        with
                pencil
                      on
                              paper

slowing down
        to catch up with
                now

Each letter written
        a commitment to
                being present

A thought lost
        creates space for
                fresh thinking

Why Are We Here?

What if the big mysteries
        weren't so mysterious?

What if we're just looking for clarity
        in the wrong places?

No Bullshit

The closer you get to
        the scorching heat of
                truth

The more bullshit
        and falsehoods
                burn away

Auntie EM – [Word Purists Beware] (1:42am)

Embodied

Emminded

Emhearted

Why not?

Wild & Free

No longer limited
by the constraints of his body
        a body that was the container of
                superior intelligence & unconditional love
my dad is now an infinite expression
of that love
        He is hurricane force winds & blazing lava heat
                untamed nature divinely organized
                      he is wild & free

Fertile Soil
(inspired by Victoria Gray)

You can't force feelings
        but…
you can cultivate conditions

When confronted with resistance
wield your trowel like a sword
plunge it into the earth of ideas
embrace with open arms
and charge forth

Leave your soft footprints as a map
for others to follow
Forge a path through the wild vegetation of thoughtlessness to
create a landscape fertile for the rise of reason

It will take an army of combat-boot-wearing feelers to pave this path
Don't be distracted by the ferocity of the footwear
It is only to protect your feet from the thorny, invasive undergrowth
of ignorance

When the earth opens and
we find ourselves once again connected
no feelings will need be forced

Namaste

At what age do we stop remembering our own divine light?

Is there a moment when we forget the marvel of being born?

We see a baby and delight in the miracle of her personhood yet
when that same baby reaches a certain age, she becomes a plebian
just another example of human failures and flaws.

Rather than expanding in the brightness of divine light
we opt to shrink into the shadows of perception

I live in this confusion
Curious about the light that flickers & shines within my body's walls
Feeling that divine spark yet daily dousing it with dark waters until
Its shimmering nature, its bright mission
reignites through the glistening lights in others

Fiery Sky

The sky was on fire tonight
telling a story rich with color and line
told from a language of light

The lens with which I made this
capture
was temporary
a pale copy stored in shadows of
my memory
to access for perspective or to simply
rest in its beauty

Beauty
a mundane word for such
majesty

Hearts & Hands

The clear suffering in the world
pierces my bubble of safety, daily
reminding me to stand firm on the
gravelly ground of now

      Balance is found in the falling
      Strength, in the wounds
      Love, in the heart of sadness

When I look around
faces betray the workings of
calloused hands that work with open hearts
looking to build a world
which honors our scars and holds us tenderly
      providing a rail to grab
         when unsteadiness threatens to knock us down

Landscaped from the sweat of
our own humanity
we gather to harvest

Hands graze the soil
      tilling what remains of the earth

On Our Island

In my house
it is typical for mom to break into a dance
it is expected to lend a hand to those in need
it is a daily practice to say please and thank you

It's not uncommon to break into spontaneous
song
laughter
hugging

My kids think it's natural to
follow one's heart
write poetry and sing out loud
make funny faces
imagine beyond boundaries

Welcome to our "Island of Misfit Toys"
where we celebrate outside the norms
encourage creative solutions
think that crazy is cool

On our island
we praise in gratitude
scribble outside the lines
throw all the flavors we love into the pot
and bring it to a boil

Bodhisattva

Even if I was not born a Bodhisattva*
I will live as if I were
working to see the light where
shadow threatens to obscure
to help, even when my
incarnate triggers are activated
to see the whole where
fractured pieces may be strewn
to Love every being as if
he or she sat at my soul table poised to sup

*someone who has achieved enlightenment, but who chooses to incarnate to help relieve the suffering of others (Mahayana Buddhism)

Heat

You passed me the torch
and with it
the flames
of your roaring fire
licked my face

Thank You

You give me the freedom to be me
        for the space to dance and sing
           to twirl and swoon

Thank you for not trying to tame me
        for honoring my feral aspects and
           for seeing my spark & keeping it lit

Light the Way

you say I am light
so I shine
you show me generosity
so I serve
you model encouragement
so I work hard
you guide me to the gold
so I collect it and
give it back to you

of love you say, don't be stingy
so I love freely

Watch Hand

It's not the watch
        I see
it's the wrist that was
once its perch
        and the hand
that once gave love pumps
        to tiny fingers

It's the Watch Hand we
        all vied for

The Second Hand ticks the moments
as heartbeats

Within that wrist
the pulse of
        an extraordinary life

Ding!

I am constantly being
awakened
by the alarm of
ideas

Past is Present
(Mother's Day)

The archives of memory are
        yellowed with age
        the wisdom contained
        masquerades as a sage

While in truth you see clearly
        what before you had not
        discernment of distance
        bestows a much greater lot

You bow deep to your heart
        where reason meets passion
        and honor your choices
        from deep-rooted to fashion

This life's an adventure
        unpredictable, true
        within its big challenges
        lives the most truest you

What's in a Moment?

a moment is not fixed by time
rather by circumstance
some are longer and more meaningful
than others

regardless of duration or story
it is the moment that is present

The moment before something tragic
        like the loss of a loved one
may have been filled with the
sounds of laughter
tastes of freshly baked cookies
smells of a wood burning fire
hopes of days to come

The moment after
        well
takes the senses on a different tour
one possibly filled with
sounds of crying
smells of his cologne lingering in the air
        stirring memory only accessed by scent

The space of time, however measured
is gone
sandwiched between the
timeless moments
before & after

Untamed

I do not wish
to destroy
or tame
the beast

I seek to
learn from its
origin story and embrace
its essential **Be**(ast)ing-ness

Who am I?
(after a day in NYC with mom and doc appts, bloodwork & scans)

I am not my hair
but my wild curls tell an
epic tale and make me smile

I am not my voice
but its vibrations
sooth the edges of sound
and make me smile

I am not my thoughts
but their persistence
amuses me
and makes me smile

Who am I?

If not the smile itself
surely I am the one
wearing it

Body Muse

slurping
burping
farting
        swallowing
        breathing
        snoring
sighing
crying
laughing
        popping
        cracking
        creaking

a symphony of sound
music conducted from the body
a solo
an aria
a monologue
a conversation

set to the rhythm of a heartbeat
        the melodies of sound
the pace of a circulatory dance
        blood travels through its narrow tunnels
        breath animates and supports the frame
ebbing and flowing
moving through time and space
indifferent to the external world
        but for the space it holds
        for the form to flow

when the sounds cease
the body returns to its source
in the stillness
        a ghostly dance
within the silence
        an echo

Guided by Voices

I remember his voice, matter-of-fact
"You're a poet."
Oh, I thought.
I'm a poet.

Then, there was the time she saw me
for who I was.
Oh, I thought.
I'm a Yoga teacher.

Years ago
it seems another lifetime
he told me I was one of his
best friends.
Oh, I thought.
And now you are one of mine.

Never limited by the labels
rather liberated by the possibilities

When our own lens is foggy
clarity may be revealed in
simple words
from those we love
guiding, not pushing
in a direction otherwise
obscured

Oh, I thought.
I am awake.
So I woke up.

Be Happy, Take Five

Take five
to feel alive

Listen to a softer sound
Find a spot and look around
Taste the goodness
Smell the breeze
Light your fire
If you please

a moment can be
short or long
depending on your
dance and song
move your body
raise your voice
deep happiness
is a choice

Perspective

Day cannot help darkening
        into night
The fiery heat of the sun
        blazes its life-giving fury
        shining its rays on all
        that grows
Nocturnal shadows
        invite rest
Within that quiet space
        lies truth
It is not my nature to
        be silent

The light of my words
        like the sun
        sets in the obscurity of
        ignorance and fear
        revealing veracity of
        an unsettling sort
In the tranquility of
        my mind
        agitation begins to stir
        a symbol of work to
        be done

Dawn brings with it new waves
        of hope
Nature's wisdom is greater than
        human ambition
        it will survive all manner of

   greed-born destruction
   without judgment or bias
It will endure

Our puny individual pursuits
   morph into a collective
   universal mission
   leaving us in the wake of
Divine dynamism
   a humbling token of
   control's illusion and
   reminder of how small we
   really are.

Wild Thing

what is it about a
Wild Thing
that stirs the cauldron of
imagination?

tickling the edges of
serenity
it taunts reason with its
unpredictable charms

rip the
virtual velvet
red rope
suspended for safety
to explore the
chasm of the untamed

what waits on the other side
is less curious than simply
dipping
swirling
treading
in its tremulous waters

Break a Leg

There is no role for
      self-righteousness in
    this play

Bleeding

My bleeding heart flows liberally
It carries in its platelets
liberty and justice for all
inclusion and Divine devotion
purpose and forward motion
clotting when the alarm bells of
dread and panic ring threatening
to obstruct its way
dissolving within the tender
nature of unconditional love

My bleeding heart is breaking
oozing from fissures of fear
dripping into the expanding pool
of growing concern
Not to drown
Not to drown
Not to drown
sucked into the depths of despair
seeing what is to be while others
whistle with carefree confidence that
all is okay

All is not okay
Drenched,
I cradle my bleeding heart in
my endless reserves
love begotten by love
creates more love
That is my mission

Love is the antidote to fear
It caulks the cracks and
fires the clay of creation
making us whole

Awakening

Ripe for awakening
I hunt for my tree
the one under which
enlightenment will unfold
I wander from plot to plot
squinting when eyes should be wide
scrutinizing in place of surrender
questioning time, place and purpose
A spatial spiritual nomad
mindful movements melt
I stop searching

Exhausted from the journey
I sit
mind chatter settles
planting thoughts
in the soil beneath my seat
to be reaped when fully formed
lest they coalesce with the earth
creating nutrient-rich ground upon which to ponder

Nurtured by the simplicity of the process
challenged by its inherent obstacles
I release
Not ripe, but ripening
a maze of single steps lies before me
offering the low hanging fruit of the path
to guide my feet
I begin

Shadow Diving

Our shadows follow us
unrelenting in their attachment
Brightness may shrink their visibility or
cast wider expressions
So be careful where you play
the light

Confusion and illusion are omnipresent
leading us to haughtiness and judgment
which are often reflections of our own
true selves

The harsher the criticism outward
the more likely the gaze should be inward
I tread lightly, knowing my own complicity
in taking my shadow by the hand
mistaking it for moral high ground
while it remains an unopened invitation to
dive deep into the ocean of awareness

Political Theatre

In a world of smoke & mirrors
what is real?

In a house of cards
where is the floor?

meandering through the
machinations of my mind
I am jolted awake by
what surely
must be
an absurd drama
playing out in the
theatre of our great land
acted to perfection on our
political stage

The playwright knows the words
yet has them jumbled
the story makes no sense
still
many in the audience seem to get it
they clap, laugh, sneer and jeer
Some get up and leave
while I and various other
lost souls
gaze around
wide-eyed and weary
waiting anxiously for the
curtain to drop

Fall

I don't remember what grade
nor do I remember the subject
What sticks in the craw of memory is
that leaf
the one outside the window
directly in my line of vision
that clung to its perch long after its brethren
had succumbed to the season
and drifted to the earth

My daily anticipation
the suspense
would the leaf – my leaf
remain fastened to its brittle branch
swinging, flowing, lolling in the breeze
Or would it have
joined its leafy friends
in the natural order?

Pocono Lake

1.

The red chairs
a visual & visceral contrast
against the lush greens that surround them
        Empty
                for now
        they wait
as the water licks the shore

2.

The lake percolates
        rippling
        bubbling
        moving
under a still blue sky
                Tall grasses
            dance to the rhythm of the breeze
catching the random Dragon or Butter –fly

3.

The presence of humans on
        kayaks
        boats
        paddleboards

adds depth to the natural context
                        sounds of laughter and
                    kids giggling
        hurl bushels of joy into the mix

4.

Wild Ferns and
Pebbled path
            pepper the way
defining with clarity
            Divine structures and
eternity with no form to contain it

The Heart of Beauty

Where does beauty live?
In the eyes, hair, smile?
If not cultivated and grown
from the heart
can it be true?

I didn't choose to change my smile
gaping hole did not make me
less whole
It taught me that humor is not
limited to things that are
funny
but that relying on exterior
is inferior
to residing beneath the
surface

Vanity forces me to
play
to tease myself silly
and share
vulnerability
To use what I have to
model for my
daughters
that beauty and humor
don't need a
groomer
that courage and
intelligence

a light step and big heart
are the biggest and truest
forms of
art

PART 1:
Still Life Performance Art

What is there to mention
about a face carved into
wood?
Wild or mild
I cannot **say**;
        perhaps the words
would be the same
as one molded out of
clay?

They breathe and
live
through an artist's **hand**
imagination and heart
at the world's
command

Reminding us
there's more to **see**
in the earth that holds us
and any random
tree

Looking deeper
beneath the **surface**
to witness a greater
vision
        It's likely, too

if you surrender
you may find
a grander
purpose

All of this you ask
from some
whittled bark
and ingredients of
soil?
My nod is silent
but my answer loud
as if this truth were
something
royal

PART 2:
Still Life Performance Art

its gaze is fixed
carved in living pulp
solid in its splintered form
we connect through the
natural world

stripped of its bark
grooves create
expression
naked
bold

ageless
yet old
deep lines hold
wisdom
from an ancient
fold

meeting us
here
now
shifting our sights
its ancient
delights
etched lovingly
in the winds of
change

Have Courage

Without sadness & fear
there would be no use for
courage

Living Mystery

fear
holds me in its grip
my body whispering
secrets
in a language I don't yet understand
I bow my head deep to hear
to listen to the roaring silence in the
spaces between the tingling

numb
I dig my nails hard into my flesh
gouging the surface to
feel
what arises is sensation
without definition
questions of Being
lasting
longing
lamenting

resilient
I lift my head high
ready
to forge forward
study the elements and
live fully in the
mystery

Book Smart

If you have a book
she says
you will never be bored

if you are reading a book
she says
you will always have something
to talk about

If you read
she knows
you will be a force in the world

Tick Tock

They're leaving
one by one

The end of the road
which was once out of sight
which once seemed infinite
which once felt solid
winding
cascading
slippery
steep
is now in clear view

The witness
no longer passive
must facilitate
administer a love so fierce
it pierces fear
All parties dread this part
there is no escape
just acceptance

Silence is the demon of grief
stillness its partner
action is distraction
but is as temporary as the moment
fleeting
heartache is waiting to
guide

teach
comfort

Time
they say "time"
it will take time
tick tock tick tock
tick…
tock…
tick…
I wait for the next "tock"
and wait
and wait
it arrives in a dew drop of clarity
and dissolves into
the primordial sound

Aunt Gail

The cigarette dangled from her
perfectly glossed lips
held the form for a moment then
released the smoke
it flowed in a stream
lingered in swirls and
dissipated into the air
From my perspective
low to the ground, looking up
I was hypnotized by this ritual

This goddess
her slim form
draped in carefully chosen fabric
moved in museum quality shoes
more arty than comfy
she took in the beauty of the world
around her including the
cute waiters
cute gallery owners
cute doctors

Her perfectly manicured nails
tipped her long fingers and loving hands
which held a glass of clear liquid
lots of ice and
lots of limes
Gin? Vodka?
Who remembers?

Over time the smoke disappeared completely
but the glass remained
along with her appreciation of cute guys and
fierce love for those she held close
Her outer aesthetic reflected her creative soul
countless canvases revealing her rich inner life

The world, her palette
Her family & friends, breath
Her art, a way to express it all

The last time I saw her
spirits were replaced by a coke with ice
she sipped slowly through a straw
pausing as the coughing consumed her
Connecting through small moments
remembering bigger times

Like the smoke of that
youthful, ageless time
when the road seemed long
the end somewhere out of sight
you held my rapt attention
and then you were gone

Capture

Nature
Love
Life
Death
Poetry's muses

words fall short of description of…
the color of the late afternoon sun reflected on autumn leaves
that feeling just before a first kiss
moving into the flow of purpose
holding the space for sorrow

yet we continue to
write
create
build
destroy
hoping to convey the essence of that pivotal moment
artfully constructing an experience to share that which
ultimately
we must know
alone

Generosity

Don't be stingy with your praise
it has the power to transform
to raise to the heights
that which is low or has fallen

Don't be stingy with your love
its magic makes full the need
leaving *wanting* to the dust of the past
and *regret* to the wind's force

Don't be stingy with your wisdom
for experience shapes us both
from the doing and the retelling
words given breath from the courage to
live fully this life

Love

I Love love
in all its parts
I love Love

I love being loved and
having loved and
loving back

Something is lovely
because it's loved
Being loving
makes everything
glow

The lover loves
and loves some more
To all the things
I have yet to love
I love you already!

How to Say It
Part 1:

When the toxicity
of words
overwhelms their
content
there is
little hope for
communication

How to Say It
Part 2:

meeting emotion with reason is combustible
when agitated
the generally dormant duo awaken
passion blocks logic
amplifying the resonance of rage
as it bounces off the walls
of fury

when dawn inevitably ignites the night sky
the sun of sanity
slowly ascends
burning through the din of darkness
like raindrops that
cleanse the earth and air
order is restored

Presence
(from a scrap paper that must have been written on shortly before my dad died)

My intention is simple
to be with what is
to sit with you
to allow the unfolding to occur
and to be present as
participant and
witness
until your final breath

Good Grief
(also written from the scrap paper following dad's physical death)

In my grief
let me feel the joy
I will not feign sadness
or create any picture of what
my heartache looks like
to make you feel better
Nor will I stop the flow of tears
when they fall

My grief is a ribbon
to unfold, unwind, untie
in my time – not yours
For those concerned
I promise I will not forget
to grieve
My grief
My way

The ebbs
are as beautiful and
meaningful as
the flows
What the waves
roll out to sea
will most certainly wash back
to shore

Freedom

My mind is well traveled
it is not confined to my body
it inhabits the past
going to places I've been
It creeps into my
dreams
to push the boundaries of the
known world
It rests behind my eyes
softly gazing into
what can be seen

I feel it
when my mind
lands in my heart
There,
it knows.
Just knows.
From my heart
my mind connects to
others through
their hearts

It moves through this
precious precarious portal
collecting passengers
creating memories
I hitch a ride
When my mind adventures
around my imagination
I am free

Body

Tiptoeing
the narrow tightrope
between heart and head
        I dip my mind
        and move my feet

Ego is of the body
        Body of thought
        Body of work

The balancing act is tenuous
bowing to my fragile self
        sometimes makes me teeter
I must surrender this identity
        without giving it away
Declare & retain it
        without a sense of ownership

What are thoughts anyway?
        Fleeting conceptual edifices
Work?
        Structures built to be destroyed
If Ego lives in these bodies
It too is a vague construct

If I am to tow this line
I must also erase it

-Ism Shmism

How narrow is your –ism?
does your femin-ism include
ladies who lunch?

Why –ism at all?

-isms tend to support belief systems
beliefs are limiting and
systems are built to keep them running

I say we tear down the –ism wall
and run wild on the other side where
it may not be greener but
it is definitely freer

Blowing in the Breeze

Lolled by an ancient tune
riding the breeze from yesteryear
I am transported to another dimension
memories draw shapes of vaguely familiar
figures
known only when called upon to
draw outside the lines of now

Scribbling
I hasten to make sense of
what I see
Words create confusion yet
the feeling persists and persists
Reason is burned away
leaving only the ash of
sensation
The melody resumes
blowing its wisdom into the wind

The Language of Feeling

Pulled in different
directions
placed in boxes labeling
others
I defy these acts
as a thinking
feeling being

The language meant to
communicate and unite
our thoughts is
divisive by nature

Open to interpretation
defined by an unshared
meaning
What's left?

The feeling

Don't Give Your Power Away

I see myself as a
dreamer

I see myself as a
warrior and a
healer
someone who is strong and
soft
smart & naïve
loving and fierce

I default to my heart
yet know discernment

I am speaker & listener both
understander* & knower
lover & fighter

The light that shines bright
within this vessel also
casts a long shadow

Every identification earned
Not to be taken by force or
desire

* made up word for poetic purposes

Fandom

I am a prostitute
I am willing to exchange coin
      for a fleeting moment of pleasure

Connection?
Define connection.
      chemistry?
           meaningful exchange of words, ideas, revelations?
                personal details that fill out the spaces between
                your respective lines?
No
none of that
Loud music and chaos
      play the part of the red velvet rope
      prevent entry to the exclusive abode of
           heart & mind
Leaving me feeling giddy and tingling
      and empty

I sit with the emptiness and ponder

What comes from this contemplation
      is a clarity rationalized by desire
The longing passes into time's tunnel
      leaving me miles from where I began yet
           right where I started

Love's Power

Love is my
sword & shield
It cuts into falsehoods
and slices illusion
It is my protection
against fear and
warmth in cool
climates

Love is the frequency
of my heart steadying
vibrations when they are
disparate and unyielding

It is my soft embrace of the world
expressed through the
exposed rawness of its purity

Seat of the Student

I don't teach because I
know the most
I teach because I
want to learn more

the seat of the teacher is
what gives
voice to the study
practice to the art
play for the soul

The seat of the teacher is
the seat of the student

Enchantment

My belief in magic is not limited to
    supernatural vibrations
        though my spirit sprinkles
            fairy dust
                on all who whose hearts are
                    open to receive

It extends to the alchemy of love to
    make golden what has dulled
        the transformational ability of friendship to
            reveal deeply rooted connection
                the gift of sadness to
                    break us wide open to
                        the golden shadows
                          which light
                          our way

Union

I do not wish to vilify you
I want to know your heart
opposition's not a deal breaker
It's a wonderful place to start

Are you willing to acquaint yourself
with the workings of my mind?
To find our common goals & dreams
leaving no stone or gem behind

If we can come together
put our differences aside
our world may evolve around us
in unity we will abide

United We Stand

United We Stand
three non-partisan words
crafted in truth without
judgement or agenda

United We Stand
is an invitation
meeting us where we are
encouraging dialogue
reminding us we are
one

United We Stand
rings archaic in the
distinct division
validations of illusion
reinforcements of separateness
we are sitting in today

United We Stand
does not require we
agree
it only asks for harmony
in our efforts
What is harmony?
Lines of music that
somehow work together
often creating something
beautiful and
unexpected

We are Falling in Division
unable to see
beyond our own beliefs
Policy & prejudice have
intertwined into a rope
knotted into a noose
poised to hang the freedoms
hard won by generations that
understood…
United We Stand!

Three Doors ~ past portals to future findings

What seems like an
impenetrable barrier is
really a doorway to
deeper understanding

On the other side
lives that which happens to
other people – strangers
joy, sorrow
vitality, disease

As long as that door
remains closed, those
others remain
separate

A moment of
clarity
reveals the location of
the doorknob
Now to find the courage
to turn the handle

Passing through the
First Portal
I am led to another
partition – this one is
made of glass

Transparent yet solid
it allows me a glimpse of
the human condition as it
lands in and on the
people I love most

Closer
clearly visible yet
still separate
I am a witness
senses dull but
awareness heightened

The glass shatters
illusions of "other" reflected
in the sharp, clear shards
leaving only a frame

I approach the third and final
opening
Stepping through this
suspended frame, it too
falls away

What's left in the
wake of this dissolution
is not separate
Lights on full
it reveals the brazen wholeness of
knowing

Scratch Paper

scribbles on scraps of paper
mini mountains of memories
context lost or obscured by time
leaving the words – their purpose & punctuation
dusty & meaningless

perhaps their power rests in the unknown
like live theatre or a potent moment
never meant to be remembered in detail
rather savored in the lingering aftertaste of the
occasion

trying to piece these fragments together
like a puzzle
to see the picture I meant to draw
when the pencil tip broke
frustrates the inscrutable urgency of
now

most of the pieces don't fit – perhaps never did
and those that create an image
are just pieces themselves
in a picture so large – perhaps infinite
its wholeness – if possible
would never fit in the limited frame
of the mind.

I pick up the nearest slip of paper
moved by the insistence of my thoughts

quickly, illegibly scratch a few words
wizard…enchantment…reality…mission

In a few years when I discover this relic
planted in the soil of creativity
will it be clear what I meant to reveal?
will it even matter?

Love Light

The house is dark
Lights flicker and dance on the snow-covered trees and pathways that surround it
making its darkness all the more
glaring
Within its walls
love, fear and hope are the bulbs that
illuminate, animate, dominate

The possibility of a White Christmas appears more possible with each new snowfall
Chimneys blow the smoke of maple and oak, filling the air with rustic charm
Holiday concerts, shopping and feelings of love and connection consume us while
smells of gingerbread and sugar cookies waft through the halls and homes
of our Norman Rockwell neighborhood

While I've never actually had Carolers come to my door
it wouldn't surprise me to hear their voices, raised in songs of praise, peace & joy,
ride the same breeze that scatters the snowflakes.

All of this draws my attention three doors down from mine
when years past this home would have had a huge wreath over the door and
lights shining their bright spirit of the season.
This year, I imagine, the house is filled with a different anticipation

Hoping and praying he makes it until Christmas
maybe even New Year's Eve.

We are not close
Friendly but not friends
Not much more than neighbors.
But, when I think about their heartache
my heart aches.
Gestures feel empty yet I yearn to find the right one.
So, I write this poem to honor his light while he is still here.
He & his family may never see these words
As vacant as this deed may be, it is my gift to the universe of impermanence
and my wish that my dear neighbors find peace in the love that is their light.

Speak Your Truth & Lighten the Load

I feel your sadness deep in the pit of my gut
It's in air and space around us
      the subtle expressions that wash over your face
      and the restrained undertones in your voice
Its ancient roots wrap around the core of joy
      fashioned at the same time and
      which inform your deepest & most basic
      truths

I tread lightly toward the beckoning heat of this core
      knowing it will be my soft landing
      following a difficult, yet necessary,
      moment of candor
I don't want to do this
I don't want to poke at vulnerability
I don't want to be the one to crack it open

I don't want to
      but I do it anyway
      understanding it is what must be
      done

The air element arrives in
      deep breaths, sighs & sobs
The water element in
      tears

The flames lick at our respective
    will
    burn away façade
    leaving a pile of ashes from which our phoenix will
    one day
    rise
Exhausted and renewed by the discomfort of this
    effort
    the earth keeps us steady

Having unburdened the load of accumulated
    unspoken words
    we collapse into a heap of trust and love
    years in the making
    waiting to cushion our fall

(That's Not) Charlotte

Down a long, winding driveway
in a rustic neighborhood outside of Philadelphia
in the upper, left-hand corner of the garage
was a masterfully & intricately woven web.

A stand-alone work of art
evidence of Mother Nature's charms
inspiration of myth
and this spider's mission

"Charolotte"
she cried with unabridged joy as she ran down the drive
momentum carrying her most of the way
The sparkle in her eye reflecting a magical view
belief brewing to a boil in her young heart

"That's not Charlotte," I said matter-of-factly
The youngest of four by many years, I grew up fast
leaving fairy tales on the dusty shelf of my childhood bedroom
diving into deeper pools of enchantment that did not begin with
Once Upon a Time or include talking farm animals

We bickered the way kids do when trying to prove their points
words simmered while heat rose like cartoon bubbles over our heads
until the flood of tears began
carrying with them a truth that would leave her innocence in a puddle
by her feet

I heard a stern grownup voice say, "In our house, we believe in magic"
as Lizzie's mom drew her in for a hug
Her words left a tar-like residue in my gut
weighing me down with an invisible anvil crafted in the land of legends
made real by my own thoughtless words

EB White made Charlotte real
and now my friend Lizzie and her family were caring for her
keeping her real until the laws of impermanence shifted perception

The web and story
misty memories made material again in the retelling
became a parable in my maternal mind as I weave enchantments
for my three daughters, today
making real what their dreams catch in their sticky threads
Prey for the spider of imagination

In our house we believe in magic

Being Present

video is a lie
it captures moments missed in real time
to be lived over again in a loop
fast forwarding through faultless flow
pausing on a timeless flash of flaw

Space

The space created by his passing
        is not empty
It hums in tune with the Universal Flow
        of all things
            allowing a temporal glimpse of
                eternity
            while reinforcing love without
                condition
This space surrounds me
        always
softly singing the melodies
        composed from a life well lived
            prodding me to wake up
Maybe that's why I love to sing
        finding solace in song's
            stories
            their disparate notes, rhythms, harmonies

The mundane is elevated
Mind and heart are
                free

Flow

So many open channels
Beings riding high frequencies
      stopping by to say hello
            staying to share their gifts and to drink
  coffee
  bourbon
  tea

I see and hear them
distinctly drawn by our senses yet
one in the stream of emotion and
    spirit

Cosmic Flow
      served in a martini glass
          feeds the illusion – softens the edges of
          cynicism enough to dive in head-first
          to a reality enhanced by external chatter
              bound to fade as the haze clears
    served on the waves of meditation
          clears the fog – thins the boundary enough
          to break through the cocoon head-first
          into a reality so clear
              it feels like a dream

Inspiration

Inspiration often taps me on the imagination
at night
after the kids are sleeping soundly
the kitchen is cleaned up from a day of use
        family of five moving in and out of the pantry & fridge
TV shows watched and
gentle stretches having moved through my
physical body

Tired from a full day
        the choice is clear
Succumb to sleep or
grab a pen
open up Word
        and write!

Spoiler Alert

There is no climax
Sorry for the spoiler alert
There is no one moment of release
    No one moment of
    revolution
    realization
    resistance
    revelation

Everything exists in a cycle
    moving ever toward its arc
Like a relay race
    innovation passes the torch to
    perpetuation which, in turn, passes it to
    annihilation
But please
Don't panic
This is nature

Following what we witness as
    ruin
Cosmic wisdom creates space
    like a nap or intermission
    a breather
where we can pause and
    contemplate creation

We get to start again.

The circle is infinite
expansive and limitless in its potential to grow
While there may not be that One
        Moment of truth
        Moment at the apex
We climb, stumble, reach and
get to abide in the gaps and structure
for as long as they exist – and then
imagine what comes next

Love (un)Defined

The more we define love
        put parameters around love
        decide what is and what is not love
        what we think is love
        judge what is love
Love will keep finding innovative ways to teach
        what it is to love
Those ways might challenge preexisting notions
It might be painful when love rips off the mask
        revealing the essence of love

House Blessing

You are welcome here
This is a place of refuge
Transmute negative forces into productive agents of joy
To those who enter and those who linger in this dwelling
      may you know wholeness in health, wealth and self
May love in all her many facets inhabit these walls

Be generous in making memories
Meander the moments without holding tight
Love without condition
Leave your impression in our hearts
      and footprints in the soft soil
as you move on

Our door is always open
Welcome Home

White Coat

Your white coat is like a
        blank page
        a clean slate
        a story somewhere in the middle
Its wisdom is worn in an ongoing
        splatter of blood
        flow of tears
        feral filth
The one you wear is stained by unearned arrogance
When you dismiss me
you skip chapters in the saga
creating gaps in your understanding
which seem only to reinforce your inflated sense of
        self-importance
Using the language of your trade to
        impress
        intimidate
        illuminate
only leaves me feeling empty and voiceless
My internal dialogue is an absurd, derogatory
back and forth of unspoken slurs
feeding the fancy of my trusted imaginary superhero
        superego

The Great Ones listen
They open to the same blank page with curiosity and pen in hand
ready to receive even the most minute detail
that may be a significant plot line in the story
        perhaps they know the value is in the listening
        more than what is actually said

The Great Ones know
it's not about them
and have the courage to be compassionate & release control to
    the ones stuck in the bed
        sitting in the lumpy chair by the window
        wearing holes in soles while pacing the halls

To the Great Ones in white coats everywhere
I bow
May they teach us all how to be
    boundless
    generous and
    wise
So that we may be Great

Stop

The sound of my sobbing heart
is a siren
vibrating off the walls in the
empty chamber of your sadness.

I cannot reach you there.

a whisper is too soft
a scream, too loud
to amplify the words
working to find the light of sound

I walk in circles
focusing my eyeballs
on the next step
expecting fully for the
view to change

It doesn't.

It is my perception that shifts
but that, too, is tenuous
alternately wakeful & sleepy
I keep moving.

It is only when I stop
that I see you clearly

Jezebel

You know you're sexier than you are pretty
           he said to my fifteen-year-old self (barely sixteen, himself)
What?
Okay, I'll take it.
Sexy works for me.

You know you're marriage material
           said my friend's boyfriend to me in my twenties
What?
That's nice to hear
But who the fuck are you to be the one to say it?!

You know you're Jezebel
           he said unwaveringly to me in my middle age
What?
My righteous indignation triggered
Disbelief registering on my face, while
Something in my soul softened
informing a deeper resonance in
my heart of understanding

Grisping
(somewhere at the crossroads of gripping and grasping)

fear worked its way into the space where faith once lived
I didn't notice it as it was happening, but
realization
once revealed
was clear

tested by moments of truth
words fail to move my feet in the direction of
what I believe
what my soul knows
what I'm waiting to surrender

it's a slow burn to purify this dread

Protest Song

I am not rallying today
but my heart beats to the rhythm of the march

My feet may not be moving with the herd of like-hearted,
like-minded protesters
but my activist soul is raised in vibration and solidarity with the message
Not so long ago it would have been unthinkable to abstain
The grays I proudly abided in would morph to black & white
no choice
no voice
leaving me stuck in some notion of absolute right-ness

With the possible exception of love
there is no such thing
It is love, in various forms and definitions, that keeps me home today

I long to add my physical body to the pack
to leave my footprints on the earth and impressions in history's log
But, today my demonstration, no less fierce, will be to hold the space for dissent,
to keep the fire of freedom lit through my words, thoughts, actions
and commitment to the bigger good

Meaning is not measured by one day
The impetus to do good is a daily call to action
It is the whisper of conscience that keeps us marching

Quest

The voice is getting louder
messages pouring in from every direction
expansive mind creates space for more to drop in
every day invites me to dance in the illuminated
rays of big hearted intelligence, while
stepping on and around the shadows of limited thinking

The voice, now a constant ringing in my ears
and behind my eyes
sings to me during challenging times of change
what once appeared to me as strength
reluctantly moves into fierce vulnerability
where courage waits to carry me home

Have Courage

The words flow with ease
        Have Courage
The breath that carries these words deepens
before shutting down
holding fear at its depth
until it is released through sound

once liberated
this beast of burden helps me to
carry the load
before purifying it in the
molten mettle of my mind

        Have Courage
is my lineage
it is my birthright
it is the carrier of completeness

Celebrating a Birthday in Heaven, Here on Earth

love and memory are entwined
infusing the air with the breath of life
braiding the seen and unseen into a rope
knotted by the past to
climb in the present for
glimpses of the future

the turning of time spins recollection
molding the clay of days into a vessel which
holds the palpable grief of loss in the same space as the
mysterious bliss of devotion and wonder

you live vibrantly in the rope and vessel
artifacts of existence
reminders of impermanence
inspiration to never stop ascending or
risking the raw exposure to the full range of emotions

Love is...

Love is
better written than any Hallmark card
sweeter than any chocolate
softer and more vibrant than the most perfect rose
Love is
measured in moments
free for all
and when shared liberally, creates abundance
Love is
the answer to the biggest mysteries

80/50 thirty years

Tiny toes touch the ground, taking wobbly first steps
My silly smile riding the momentum, secure in your loving hands
I can conquer this walking thing and meet every future challenge
with wonder & curiosity,
knowing your strong soft hands and steady stance will support me
as we alternate who takes the lead

Cutting the foggy floor of teenage angst
Stepping forward into the future
Dipping down to the depths of confusion
Rocking to the beat of the City
Holding loved ones close
Swaying with the winds of change

We twirl, tap, tango into our fuller selves with every year – continuously progressing, expanding. What remains constant is love

No need for a formal dancefloor, just the music and my mom – our collective souls
caught in the joy of the dance – we are timeless.

Your heartbeat - my first experience with rhythm
I moved when you moved, cradled in the safety of your womb
When you danced, I danced, and we've been dancing together ever since!

New Traditions

wiping up the virtual crumbs of matzah never consumed
swaying to memories of
        songs unsung
        rituals revised
        secret smiles
anticipating hidden eggs of every color, to be pursued later by eager seekers
sisters plot their course, giggling
        nature calls to explore her trails
        emotions pass from heart to hands
        April's fool never to be found

Spring Snow

The lamb does not pass the lion in March, as we wake to
        another Spring Snow

Like the bear in winter, my instinct is to remain asleep but
        the promise of Springtime
              with its warmer temperatures
      soft raindrops and
      earth splitting open with new life
      beckons my body to rise – to
Break through the ground of my own complacency
Imagine that which cannot be seen
Grow toward the sun, which
        for the moment remains hibernating behind a white sky

It too will emerge and shine to fulfill Spring's promise

Marble

There are faces in the marble
formed by blue veins that run through the rock
      they are reminders to look closely at the world
          so that I may see
not only the mysteries and subtleties that live between blinks, but
      the beauty and simplicity of this natural world

They, of course, are permanent in their grins and smirks,
so when it appears they have altered expression,
      I must look at my own reflection for that change
Amused by this silent audience, I regard the shapes as mini mirrors
      comfort, clarity, comic relief – empty or full, they reveal
a piece of the story
and the wonder of discovery

When Words Fail

I am elevated by mother nature's poetry
    and wish to write of her structures and creatures
        the majesty of her seasonal wisdom and selfless gifts
            to explore the Mother/Human Nature relationship
        from an elemental perspective

But my mind often wanders
    getting lost in the neighborhood of ideas
        leaving my footprints in the supple, questionable soil of
        life's meaning

In my quest for understanding, nature and nurture mingle
        inviting the vastness of the universe into the realm of
        humanity
            wondering where in this space choice lives & how
            consequences are doled out

        Soft rain falls from the sky
        absorbed quickly by the thirsty earth
        Elsewhere, lightening strikes an old tree
        cracking it to its core
        In the beyond, a field of daisies spring to life
        dotting the landscape with their friendly petals

        Words can scarcely describe the experience of a flower

Shake it Out

I gingerly step out of the shower
unexpectedly, yet vigorously, moving my head quickly side to side
I shake my sopping, short, shaggy shock
releasing my locks, while spattering droplets of water
on every surface and wall around me

This wild dance is a fury of swaying strands which
slap my face and move my feet to join the party
Laughing at what feels innately canine, I hum along
with the momentum that has swelled

When stillness comes, abruptly, there is a tingling
that moves into my fingers causing them to wiggle
resonating with the spontaneous tango
I am alive

What Lies Beneath

At first I just wanted to play
flirt with highlights & lowlights
daring dyes and fantasy colors
There were hits and misses along the way but
always a sense of ephemeral playfulness

The suggestion of fall foliage woven into my tresses
absorbing and refracting the sun's rays
magnified the vision and created new colors
not found in the mortar and pestle of the salon

Still amused by this ongoing ritual, my impetus shifted
when the silver strands became more evident
Clever coverage became paramount; an artist's challenge
with years to perfect

The lightheartedness which initially informed the game
became tedious; labor rather than leisure left me longing and
curious to expose what lived beneath the surface

Patiently awaiting the big reveal, I smiled at the shimmering threads
which begged for the same sunshine to elevate their hidden hues
Perhaps in this release lies some dormant power or silent source
of awakening

Could silver strands be the new ruby red slippers?
Has the power always been in me?
If discovery uncovers a different truth, well,
there are myriad pigments still waiting to play

High Frequency

Frequencies are moving
wriggling in and out of old paradigms
magnetizing to the source
Heightened, in part, by charms of the heart
communities of soul seekers gather
Supported by unseen structures
we pass the orb of light to one another
like a candle whose eternal wax & wick
ignite the world to blaze
without diminishing its own fiery fund
Red embers of purified demons rest in the shadows
while the world pulsates to the relentless drum circle of
awakening

Tick Tock

Time stopped that day
opening the curtain to the final act of
life's greatest mystery

The steady ticking of the second hand
clicks away the days before we even
notice that the hour hand has moved

Songs unsung remain caught
in the web of dreams
waiting for the perfect moment to
escape, to liberate from the pasty threads
woven by fear and regret

When the second hand slows to
a stop, it will be too late

This flash of awareness
sets all time pieces to "now"
shreds old lists that hold in their words
excuses, rationalizations, procrastinations

Treasure the moment for what it holds
- precious gems of purpose and mission
- silent spaces held for contemplation and connection
- silliness inspired by the cosmic joke

Time stops one day
And it keeps on ticking

Waiting for Spring

Spring is shy this year, hiding behind winter, peeking out
from time to time
to let us know she's there

I walk outside and yell, "Boo!" in an attempt to coax her out to play

Feeling furtive glances from behind trees
Hearing hushed tones under the soil
Smelling sweetness in the breeze

What my senses cannot translate remains a mystery
I trust her quiet wisdom & patiently wait to play

Fuck

I've heard it be told
that words have vibrations
some higher than others
they have their own stations

I take issue with that
communication is personal
to speak direct from the heart
choose from your own word arsenal

Who made this distinction
that some words are "bad"
They're there for us all
when happy, frustrated or sad

On days that are cheery
thoughts might come out floral
When moving from solo to many
choose words that are plural

Expression is freedom
a chance to express
our myriad emotions
our ease and our stress

There are moments in life
when one can feel stuck
and nothing feels better
than just saying, FUCK!

Lost in Thought

St. Anthony, patron saint of lost things
It's your constant companion calling

You have lit dark corners
cleared cob webs and dust bunnies
directed me to see what has been concealed
And now I call upon you, once again
to lead me to what I lost
It's not a watch or cell phone, notebook or car keys
This time the reveal lies somewhere in the
maze of my mind
you see
I have misplaced a thought
A thought I clearly remember having while washing pots & pans
A thought that promised to remain until the soap was rinsed
A thought that would have replaced the words I'm writing now

If this thought
this mislaid moment
should spark your talents for tracking
you know where to find me

Role Playing

Sometimes I'm dominant as the witness
        seeing and translating the world around me from the perspective of where I am
Sometimes I'm dominant as the scribe
        taking those observations and using written words to communicate them
Sometimes I'm dominant as the actor
        the one performing the tasks of being human
        from my flawed mortal nature to the shiny ideal to which I aspire
Always my eyes are open
pen in hand
ready to take the stage

Breezy

There's something about a spring breeze as it moves through
open windows and spaces
navigating around treetops and flowerbeds
sending smells of the season to hard-to-reach places
aiding pollination as it delivers seed to receptive soil
carrying fresh possibilities on its current

Alone in the car
windows & sun roof wide open
music blaring
an unsolicited smile forms on my face
inspired by the breeze
that is my breath

What's for Breakfast?

Giggles and oatmeal
sweetened with blueberries & brown sugar
given crunch with bits of cereal
layered with mirth to raise the
electric vibration of our special bond

Cooking, feeding, nourishing
expresses a love so deep
each bite is a tasty sample of
something eternal

Crafting such a bowl of food
in the light of laughter is
joy transcendent

The empty bowl
exposes this moment's ephemerality
Echoes of laughter's vibration
subside into a soft, warm space
creating conditions for renewal

After a well-deserved nap, I ask
What would you like for lunch?

Keep Walking

Feet planted firmly in the field of intention
mind wanders, reeled in by the power of my breath

Years of practice navigating the intricate pathways of
my mind – running from and toward the light of ascension
leaves me curious to keep moving, traveling, being

Sitting tall, contained yet unrestrained within the earth
that is my body – what was once sown
begins to break through, revealing buds of clarity from
their inception with promises to continue unfoldment

Humbled by nature's wisdom when coupled with purpose
I shift attention back to the ground beneath my feet

I stand, taking sacred steps toward a planned yet
unknown destination

April 17, 2018

One year ago
I awoke
beside his
bedside
and caught his final
yet eternal
breath

Today
the breeze
inhaling essence
exhaling feeling
carries his
central being-
ness ~
wisdom & hugs
laughter & love
without condition

words fail when
memory
flicks that switch
electrifying the
dormant days
that have filled
the space
since he left

I feel the
cool touch of the

zephyr
on my skin
See it move the
leaves and
reorganize the
lawn
I see the
Red Cardinal
Dragonfly
Butterfly
Holding these
winged creatures
in my aching heart
as a sign

They glide effortlessly
on the buoyant
unseen current
that brings him
home

Coin Toss

Discipline & indulgence arrive with equal allure
satisfying in different ways
Both essential for harmonizing the
Need:Want ratio
which creates something beyond the math

Action:Stillness
Reality:Fantasy
Logic:Absurdity
Like a coin flipped in the air
landing on its edge

Which way will it fall?
Is it chance or choice that
guides the toss
Are choice:chance
just opposite sides of the
same coin?

Heaven at Home

From my comfy bed
I can clearly see the trees
Heaven is right here

Technicolor Life

I dream in color, I think
if not while I slumber
for sure when I'm awake

Drifting on the breeze of imagination
I slip smoothly into promising places
worlds reflected in the
changing seasons and
daily miracles of Mother Nature

Music fills the spaces in my mind
where vibrant hues draw lines
creating shapes that move
to the drum beat of my heart and
stimulate a deep seeded song

Clouds glide across a clear blue sky
their movement reveals stillness while
gauging the speed of flying creatures and
of fluttering leaves

A suggestion of children's play is
exposed by the colorful kite
caught high in the budding limbs
of Spring's awakening
The blue ever brighter

Not asleep yet
not quite stirring

I am alive in the reverie of
dazzling realities as they
mix together on the
palette of possibility

Water

The water bubbles on the glass
obscuring details
magnifying meaning

The water drips down the glass
changing the picture
opening perception

The water droplets on the glass
mimic the rain that falls from the sky
pooling at their respective bottoms
offering the possibility to
dance and splash
flourish, break soil & grow

This water is no different from
the water we drink
bathe & swim in
behold when ponds are slick & still
rivers and oceans, raging
It possesses the power to
hydrate and drown

Inside this microcosm
neither benign nor malevolent
resides simple truths
In its globule form
viewed from either side of the glass
we get a glimpse
an opportunity to witness a
small miracle

The Once & Future...

In the fleeting moment I glimpse my purpose
the sword glides from the stone with ease

The years of trying to coax it out through
the will of my ego
leaves the rock fractured but not broken
until it crumbles into a pile of rubble
under the pressure of fear

Sifting through the debris
like Sisyphus pushing the boulder
day after day
year after year
I found meaning in the search

My hour of consciousness arrived
The meaning I'd been pursuing
divulged in the simplicity of my breath
was the glue that re-formed the stone
my boulder

The sword's blade, gleaming
Its origin story, a wonder
I took a deep breath as my fingers
wrapped around the hilt's grip
and with a deep knowing
wielded my life's mission
with a single slice

Earth Song

Her hum fills my voice with song
it wells in my soul and pools in my heart

Salty tears flow into my open mouth
flavoring the notes I labor to sing

Vibrato quivers more than usual
choking the harmony into a burst of sound

It is a warm vibrational wash of color and fragrance
like invasive blossoms silhouetting Spring's budding foliage

Even in Her darkest moments she stands tall, proud
offering Her best to elevate us to our highest standards

Her resilience is a melody that grips the globe
sometimes forming words for us to chant in unison

Other times Her tune is an invitation to hum along
as individuals united by her song

The Gift of Emptiness

I'm on empty
scraping the bottom of the bowl of ideas for
a crumb to nibble
a fragment would be enough to nourish my
depleted vessel

The blank page taunts me
It reminds me of all the
words waiting to be written
thoughts seeking to find their form
messages lost in bottles floating on unknown waters

This may sound bleak but
I assure you it's not
It is from this place of
uncertainty
mystification
perplexity
that the complacent world is
shaken up, stirred to action
clarified on a soul level

Running on fumes now, I
sputter to the station of dreams to
refuel imagination
It is there I pause & consider the exchange
What I will trade for the promise of
feeling full

Knots

Fibers intertwine
weaving over and under
under and over
creating habitual patterns of movement until
there's no wiggle room and
advancement ceases

The more they try to move
the tighter they become
no longer resembling the vibrant strands that
organized around their casual current
They seize

What is it they hold in the
unyielding spaces in between?
Crusty bits flake off in the effort made to
untangle
un-strangle

The structure matters not
necklace
shoelace
under the left shoulder blade
in stomach's hollow
patterned on a wooden floor or
in the trunk of your favorite tree

Knots are knots are knots
some easier to unsnarl than others
Unflappable fingers can comb through the web of confusion as

breath and awareness can soften the resistance around
knitted connective tissues
Those in lumber's grain can serve as a focal point to
unwind the mind

I sit with the pit's gnarled seed in my gut
gazing hazily on the planks that make up my floor
Small swirly knots on the surface reflect the process I must endure to
uncoil
unravel
to loosen what has constricted around my flow

Giving & Receiving

Hands in fists, hold tight
no space for light to shine through
nails piercing flesh in service of the grasp
and not much more

Working hands create, mold and sculpt
write and build with pens and hammers
breaking through what we see, in service of progress
and so much more

When hands touch with love, they have the
power to heal hurts from minor scrapes & scratches to
deeper scars of loss & brokenness, in service of compassion
What more is there

When outstretched, poised to give or receive,
these hands are servants of the heart
They know that sharing goes both ways
There's grace inside the benefactor and the beneficiary, alike
in service of equanimity
There is no more

Lighten Up

When the world feels like a boa constrictor
coiling around the sources of breath
cinching the cord that connects to life
jeopardizing the existence of existence
intelligent assessment & action can sustain the moment
but laughter and silliness will release constraint

When "normal" threatens to become the custom
tap the keg of improbability to emancipate the eccentric
liberate the absurdity that rides your expanding breath and
giggle
snort
howl
cackle
tickle
tease
Treat the world with a light touch
Hold your treasure in an open palm
Model warriorship with an un-constricted heart

Nature's Secrets

It's cold again today but
please do not tell the buds
Nature is teasing them out with
cool seasonal rains and
pockets of warmth cloaked in the
shadows of passing sunbeams

Sometimes, I feel like an interloper
dropped in the wild terrain
belonging to the flora and fauna
Reflected in the watery pools of
ponds
lakes
dew drops
tears
I see clearly the truth of unity, yet
consciousness is a tricky tool

Muddled by the countless
expressions of separateness
my vision blurs as I fix my gaze
upon the sparkling water which
dispassionately leaves me to my daily quest

Suffering and flourishing share the same soil
Frost keeps seedlings underground until the
sun draws them up
Winter turns to Spring
Summer to Fall

Each cycle offering opportunity to
prosper or perish

It's cold again today but
I don't need to inform the buds
They know

What is the Purpose of a Porcupine?

Poetic pundit ponders
what is the purpose of a porcupine?
Within the probe she may find
more than principle, a divine sign

About the Author

Photo Credit:
Karen Klein-Schaffer

Sherry's dreams have always included a need for authentic connection and aspects of healing, educating and entertaining. Whether it was on stage, answering phones, collecting cover charges, checking coats, demonstrating cookware, writing or teaching yoga & meditation, these qualities have remained steady. Moved by a vivid imagination and deep reverence for the role of witness, Sherry is in a constant state of creativity and inquiry.

Wild & Free – Poetry of Living, Loving and Letting Go is the third and final collection in her "Wild" poetry series (previously published by Balboa Press, Love's Wild Journey – Poems from an Untamed Heart & Wild Fire – Poetic Prisms). Other published works include inclusion of two poems (Silent Sounds & In the Moment) in The Poetry of Yoga – A Contemporary Anthology Volume 1 (Edited by HawaH), as well as articles in local papers and online magazines.

Sherry lives in Bucks County, PA with her husband, three daughters, dog and two cats.